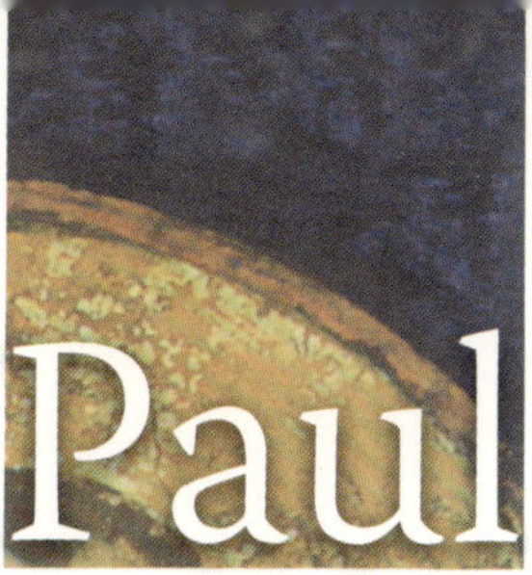

Paul

Messenger of the Good News

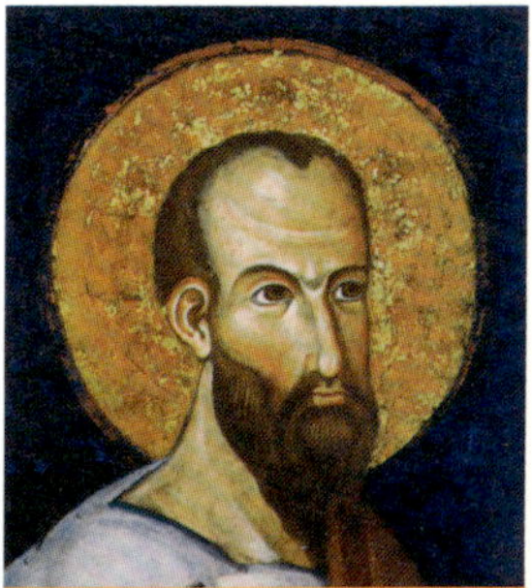

Paul
Messenger of the Good News

Illustrations from "San Paolo nell'arte contemporanea", Edizioni San Paolo, Cinisello Balsamo (MI) and the Archives of the Paoline Edizioni, Rome, Italy

ISBN 1-904785-30-4

Published in the United Kingdom in 2005
Pauline Books & Media
Slough SL3 6BS
www.pauline-uk.org

Paul
Messenger of the Good News

This is a little introduction to the life of St Paul, in his own words. It presents a vision of the apostle Paul, messenger of Jesus, builder of communities. On the occasion of our 50th anniversary of foundation in Great Britain, it seemed appropriate to us, Daughters of St Paul, to produce a homage to this great apostle from whom we draw inspiration in our efforts to spread the Good News of Jesus Christ. In the spirit of Paul, we use word, sound and colour – all forms of communication, to enable people of every nation to find for themselves an answer to their hearts' deepest questions.

So, this is Paul, speaking in his own words. You can read and pause to reflect on each page, and pray with him as well. The text is enriched with a variety of paintings by classic and contemporary masters of art – a gallery of images portraying a man who still inspires men and women of today to become heralds of the Gospel. We gratefully dedicate this to all the special people who have collaborated with us and helped us in our efforts over the past 50 years – to proclaim the Good News in Great Britain.

The Daughters of St Paul

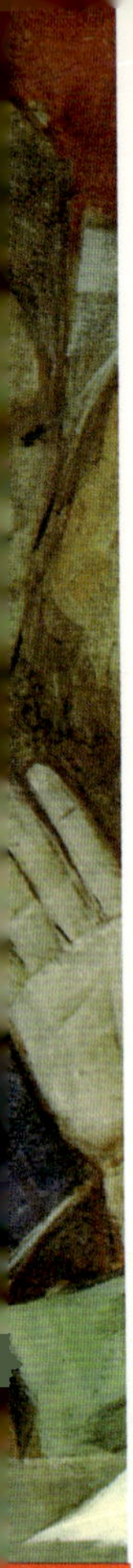

At the feet of Gamaliel

Paul: Who am I?

I am a Jew,
born in Tarsus in Cilicia,
but brought up here in this city
where I was educated in the school of Gamaliel,
according to the strict observance of our Law.
And I was dedicated to God's service,
as are all of you today.
Acts 22:3

I was circumcised when eight days old.
I was born of the race of Israel,
of the tribe of Benjamin.
I am a Hebrew, born of Hebrews.
With regard to the Law, I am a Pharisee,
and such was my zeal for the Law
that I persecuted the Church.
As for being righteous according to the Law,
I was blameless.

Philippians 3:5-6

Are they Hebrews? So am I.
Are they Israelites? So am I.
Are they descendants of Abraham? So am I.
2 Corinthians 1:22

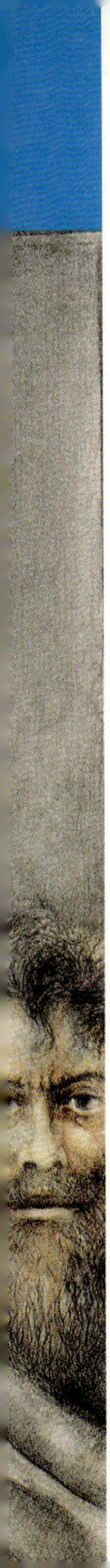

Persecutor of Christians

I myself in the beginning
thought that I had to use all possible means
to counteract the name of Jesus of Nazareth.
This I did in Jerusalem and,
with the authorisation of the chief priests,
I put in prison many who believed;
and I cast my vote
when they were condemned to death.
I went round the synagogues
and multiplied punishments against them
to force them to renounce their faith;
such was my rage against them
that I pursued them even to foreign cities.
With this purpose in mind
I went to Damascus with full authority
and commissioned by the chief priests.

Acts 26:9-12

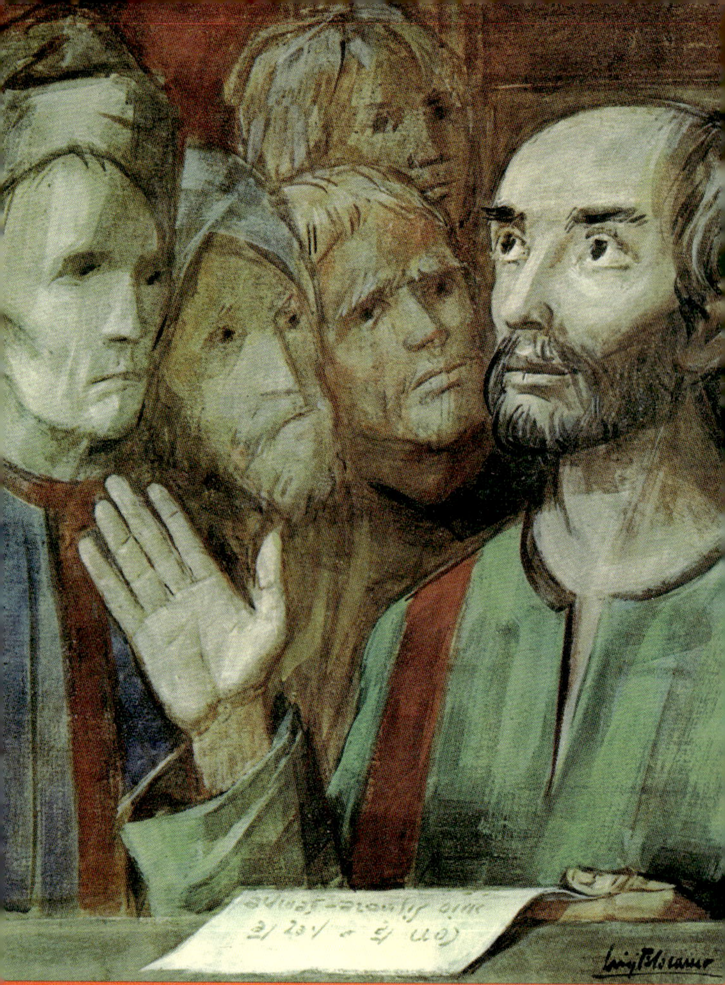

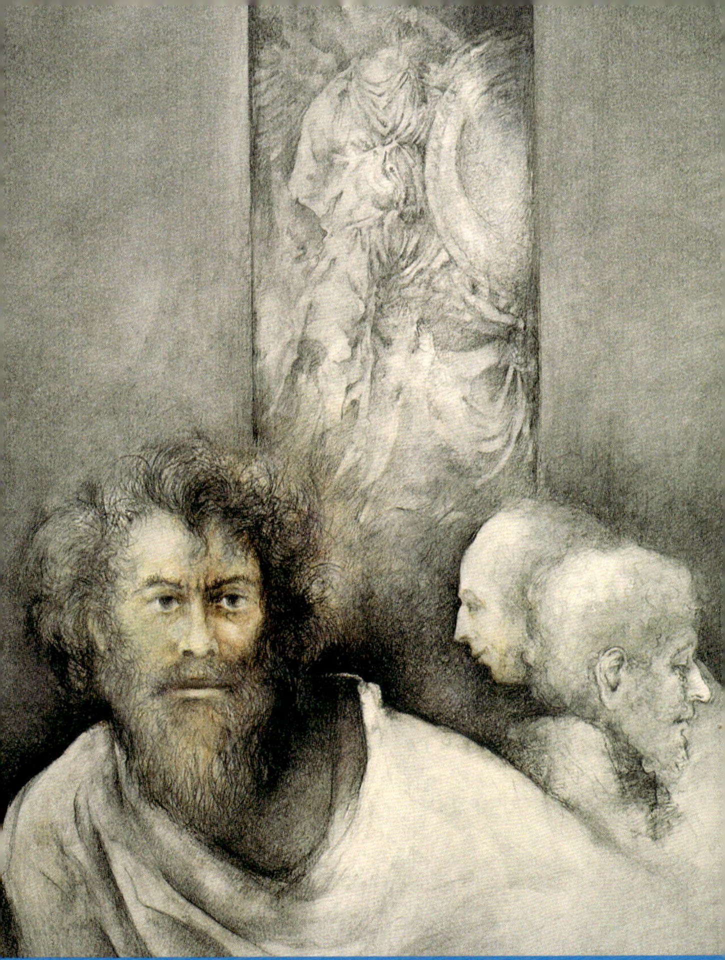

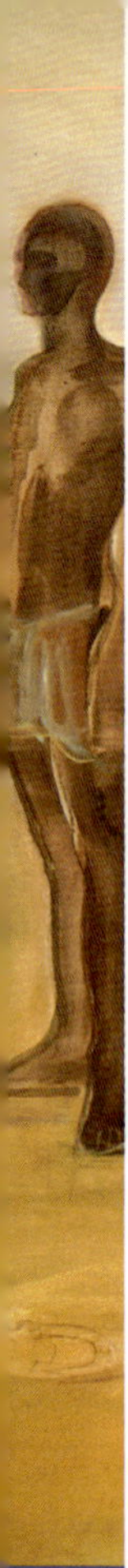

Captured by Christ

But as I was travelling along,
nearing Damascus,
at about noon a great light from the sky
suddenly flashed about me.
I fell to the ground and heard a voice saying to me:
'Saul, Saul, why do you persecute me?'
I answered: 'Who are you, Lord?'
And he said to me:
'I am Jesus the Nazarean whom you persecute'...
I asked: 'What shall I do, Lord?'
And the Lord replied: 'Get up and go to Damascus;
there you will be told
all that you are destined to do.'
Acts 22:6-10

I press on till I conquer Christ Jesus,
as I have already been conquered by him.
Philippians 3:12

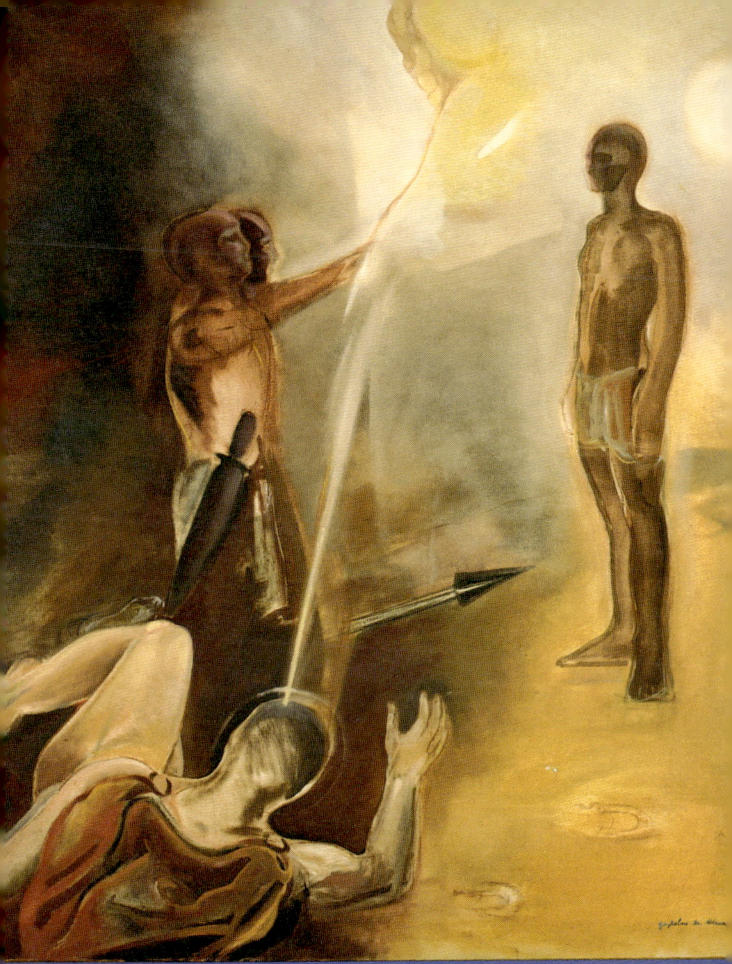

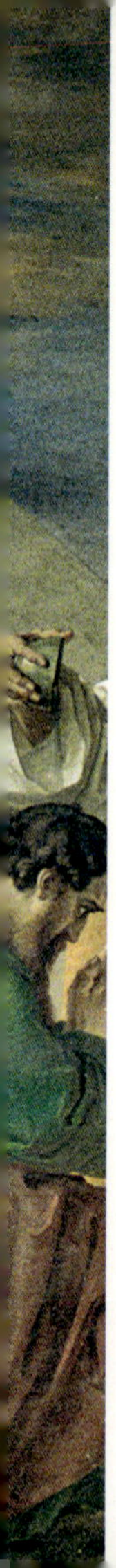

Change of mentality

There a certain Ananias came to me...
he said: 'And now, why delay?
Get up and be baptized
and have your sins washed away
by calling upon his Name.'
Acts 22:12.16

But once I found Christ,
all those things that I might have considered as profit,
I reckoned as loss.
Still more, everything seems to me as nothing
compared with the knowledge of Christ Jesus,
my Lord.
For his sake I have let everything fall away
and I now consider all as rubbish,
if I may gain Christ.
May I be found in him...
and become like him in his death,
and attain through this, God willing,
the resurrection from the dead.
Philippians 3:7-11

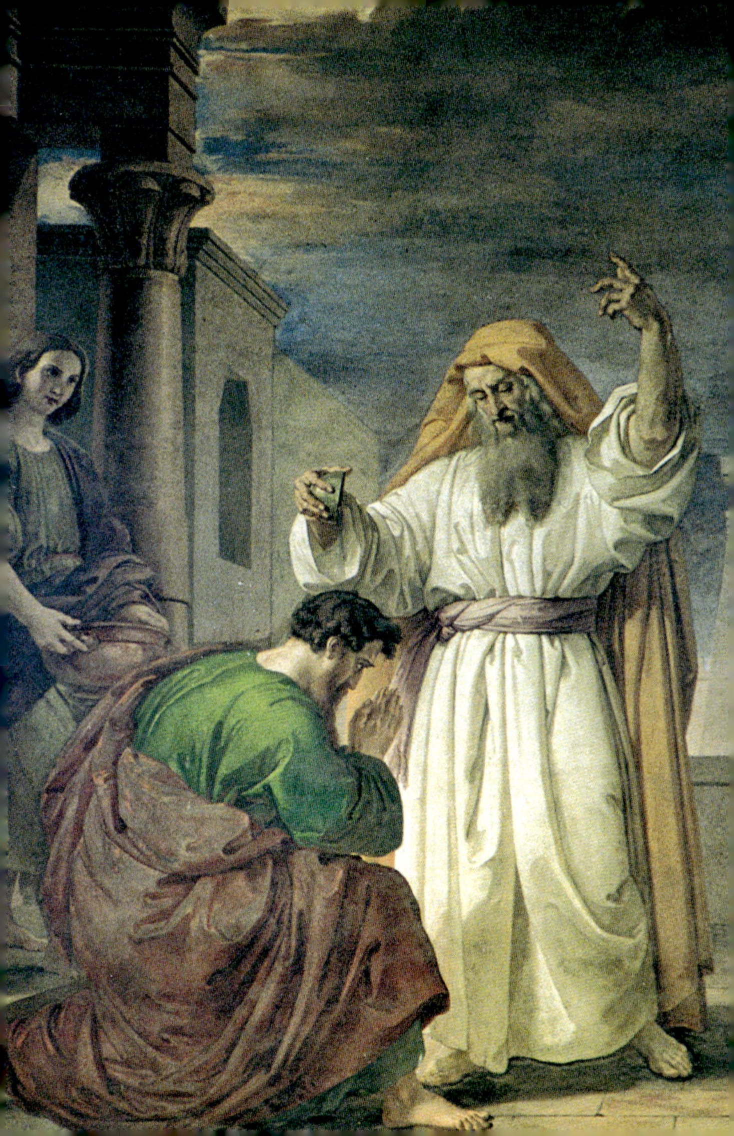

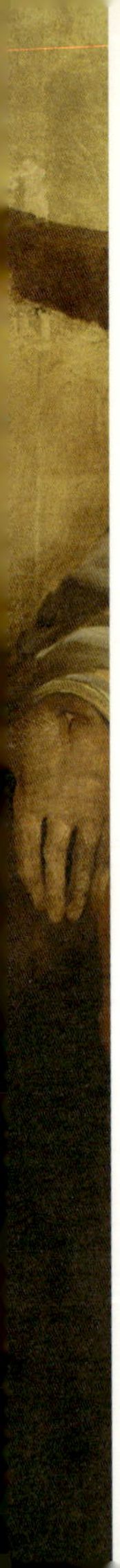

Renewed in Christ

I give thanks to Christ Jesus, our Lord,
who is my strength,
who has considered me trustworthy
and appointed me to his service,
although I have been a blasphemer,
a persecutor and a rabid enemy.

1 Timothy 1:12-14

But one day God called me,
out of his great love,
he who had chosen me from my mother's womb;
and he was pleased to reveal in me his Son,
that I might make him known
among the pagan nations.

Galatians 1:15-16

I am crucified with Christ.
Do I live? It is no longer I, Christ lives in me.
My life in this body
is life through faith in the Son of God
who loved me and gave himself for me.

Galatians 2:19-20

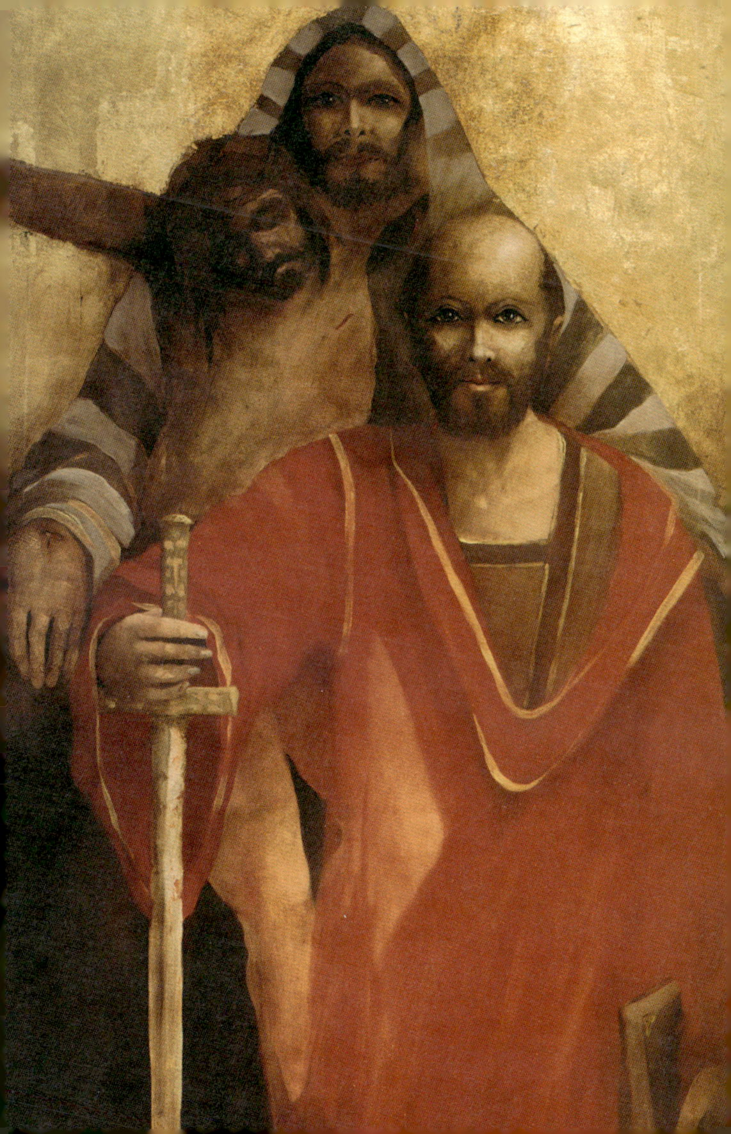

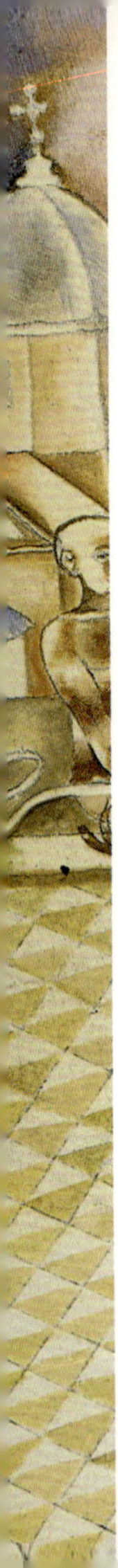

The scandal of the Cross

So then, where does that leave the wise,
the educated people, the philosophers?
And the wisdom of this world?
God let it fail.
At first God spoke the language of wisdom,
and the world did not know God through wisdom.
Then God thought of saving the believers
through the foolishness that we preach.
The Jews ask for miracles
and the Greeks for a higher knowledge,
while we proclaim the Crucified Christ.
For the Jews, what a great scandal!
And for the Greeks, what nonsense!
But he is Christ,
the power of God and the wisdom of God
for those called by God
among both Jews and Greeks.
In reality, the *foolishness* of God
is wiser than human wisdom,
and the *weakness* of God
is stronger than human strength.

1 Corinthians 1:20-25

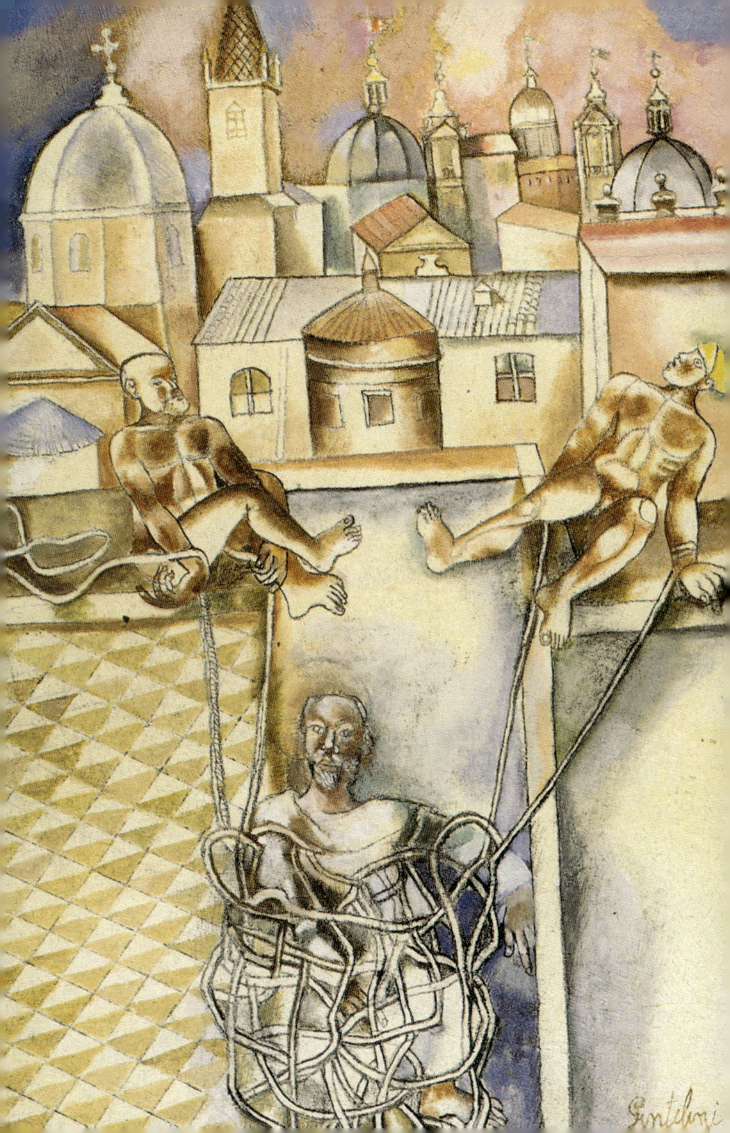

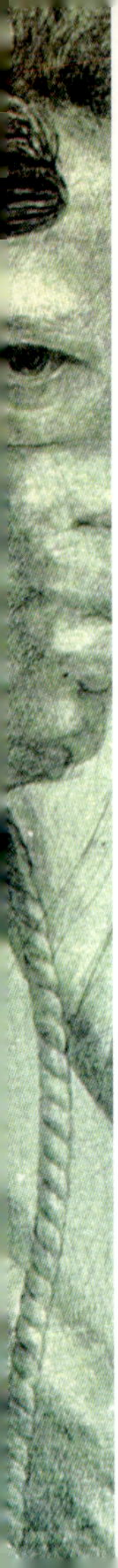

The conflict within me

In fact I do not do the good I want,
but the evil I hate.
Therefore, if I do what I do not want to do,
I am not the one striving towards evil,
but sin which is in me.
I discover, then, this reality:
though I wish to do what is right,
the evil within me asserts itself first.
My inmost self agrees
and rejoices with the law of God,
but I notice in my body another law
challenging the law of the spirit,
and delivering me as a slave
to the law of sin written in my members.
Alas, for me!
Who will free me from this being
which is only death?
Let us give thanks to God
through Jesus Christ, our Lord!

Romans 7:19-25

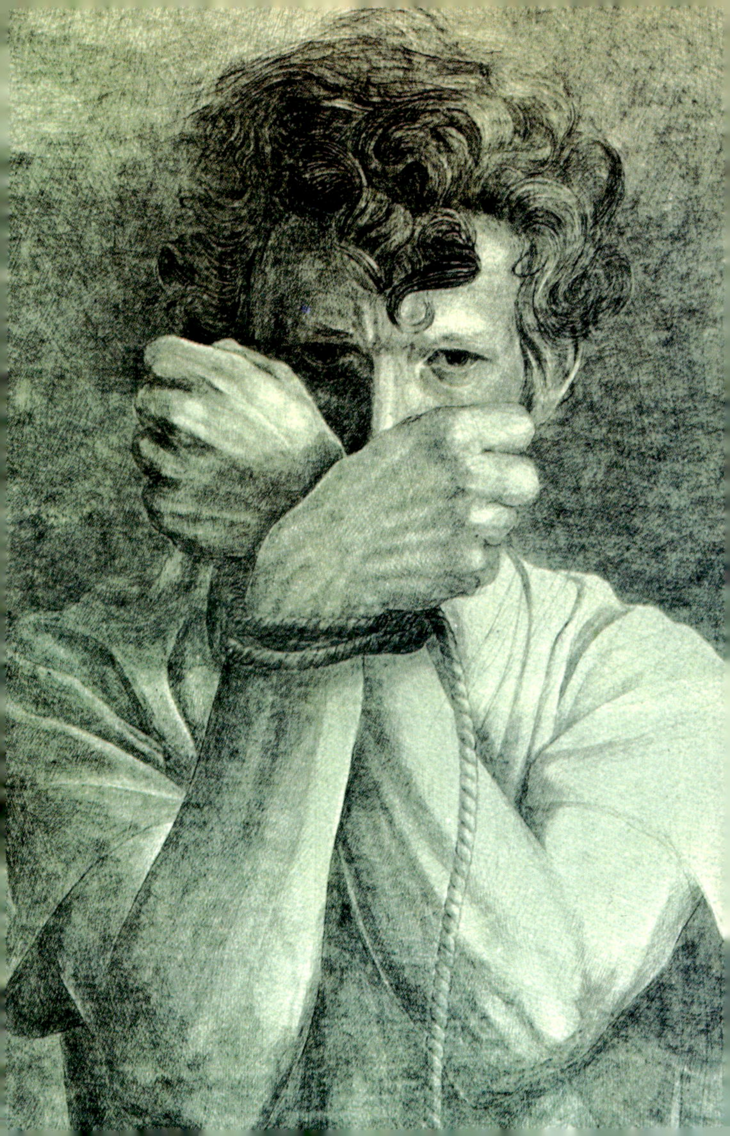

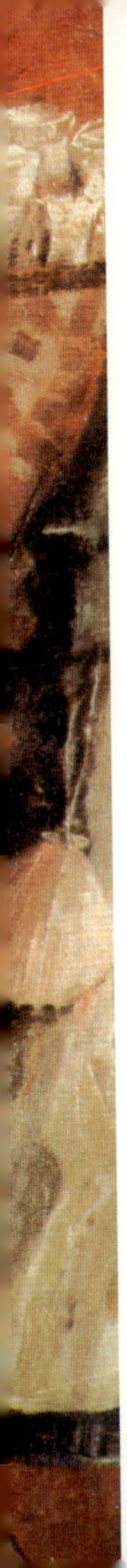

Messenger of the Good News

According to the Gospel we brought you...

1 Thessalonians 1:5

...hope does not disappoint us
because the Holy Spirit has been given to us,
pouring into our hearts the love of God.
Consider, moreover,
the time that Christ died for us:
when we were still sinners
and unable to do anything.
Few would accept to die for an upright person;
although for a very good person,
perhaps someone would dare to die.
But see how God manifested his love for us:
while we were still sinners,
Christ died for us
and we have become just through his blood.
With much more reason now
he will save us from any condemnation.

Romans 5:5-9

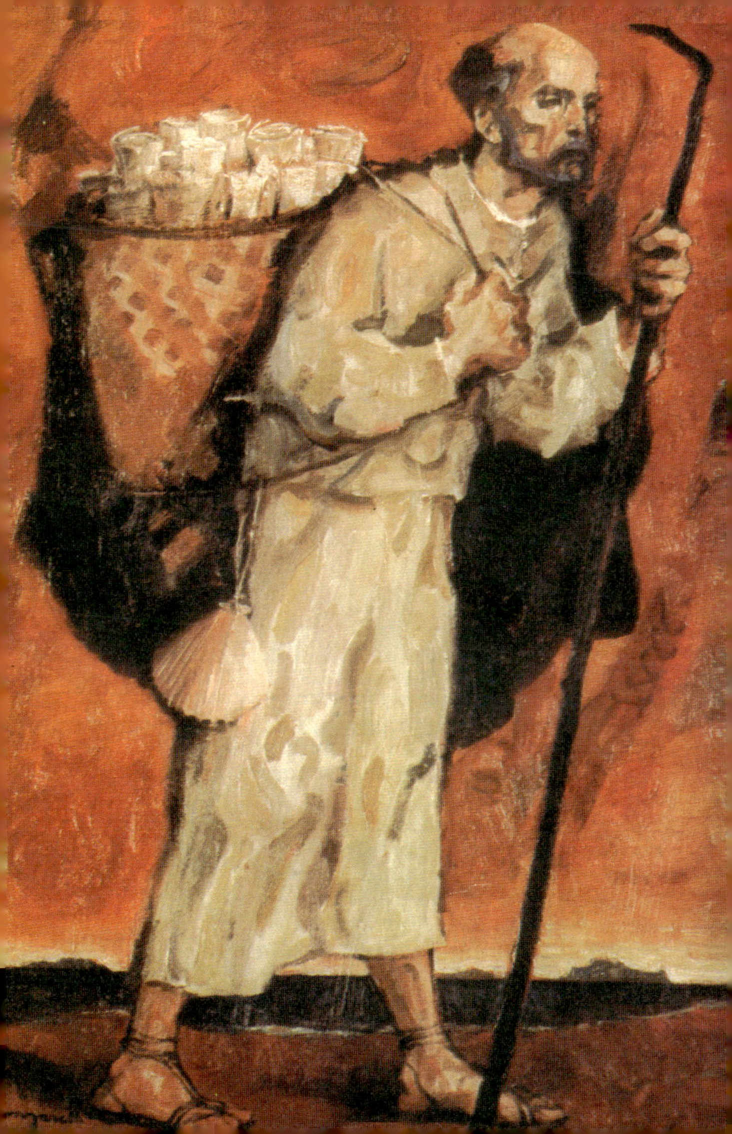

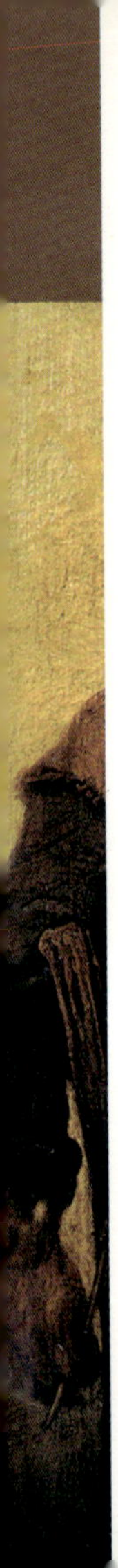

Eternal Glory

Therefore we are not discouraged.
On the contrary, while our outer being wastes away,
the inner self is renewed from day to day...
So we no longer pay attention
to the things that are seen,
but to those that are unseen,
for the things that we see last for a moment,
but that which cannot be seen is eternal.
We know that when our earthly dwelling,
or rather our tent, is destroyed,
we may count on a building from God,
a heavenly dwelling not built by human hands,
that lasts forever.
As long as we are in this earthly tent,
we indeed moan our unbearable fate
for we do not want this clothing
to be removed from us;
we would rather put the other over it,
that the mortal body may be absorbed by true life.
This is God's purpose for us, and he has given us
the Spirit as a pledge of what we are to receive.

2 Corinthians 4:16 - 5:5

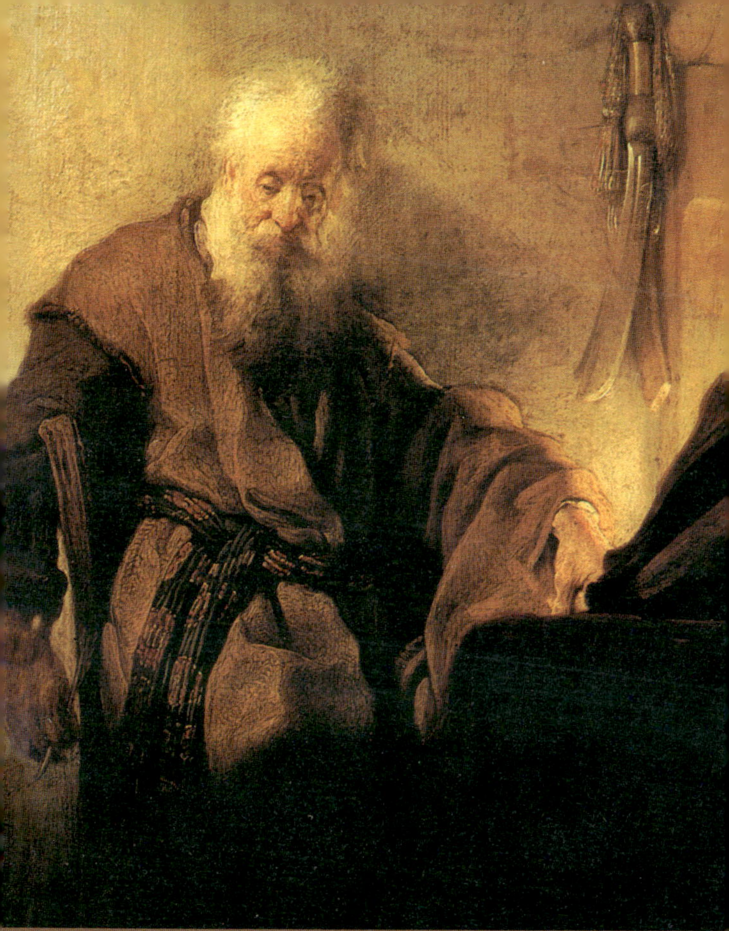

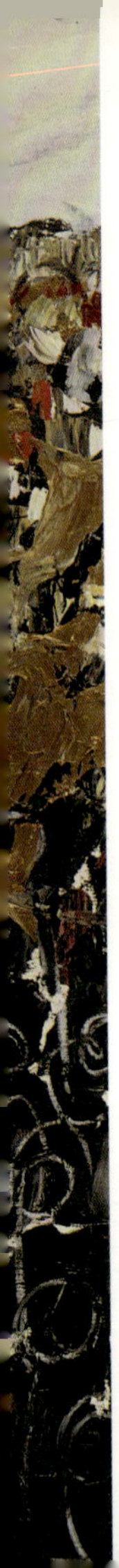

One God the Father of All

Therefore I, the prisoner of Christ,
invite you to live the vocation you have received...
Make every effort to keep among you
the unity of Spirit through bonds of peace...
one Lord, one faith, one baptism.
One God, the Father of all,
who is above all and works through all and is in all.

Ephesians 4:1-6

Now, in Christ Jesus,
all of you are sons and daughters of God
through faith...
Here there is no longer any difference
between Jew or Greek,
or between slave or free,
or between man or woman:
but all of you are one in Christ Jesus.

Galatians 3:26-28

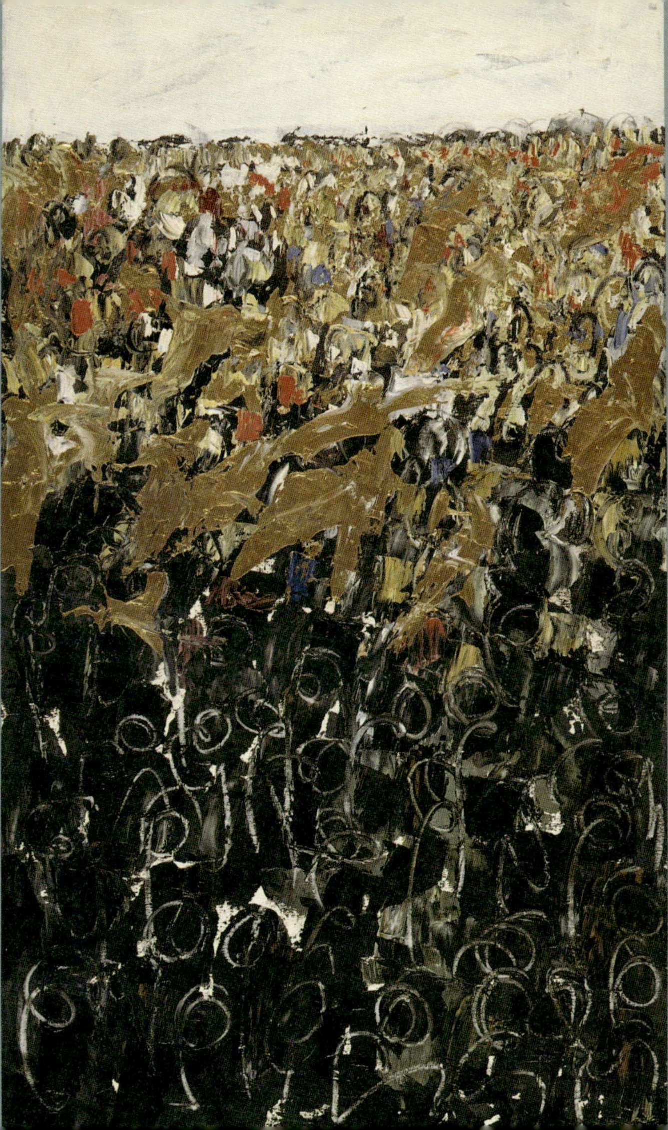

For the sake of the Gospel

Until now we hunger and thirst,
we are poorly clothed and badly treated,
while moving from place to place.
We labour, working with our hands.

1 Corinthians 4:11-12

How can I, then, deserve a reward?
In announcing the Gospel,
I will do it freely without making use of
the rights given to me by the Gospel.
So, feeling free with everybody,
I have become everybody's slave
in order to gain a greater number.
Among the weak in faith I became weak
like one of them, in order to win them.
So I made myself all things to all people
in order to save, by all possible means,
some of them.
This I do for the Gospel,
so that I, too, have a share in its blessings.

1 Corinthians 9:18-19.22-23

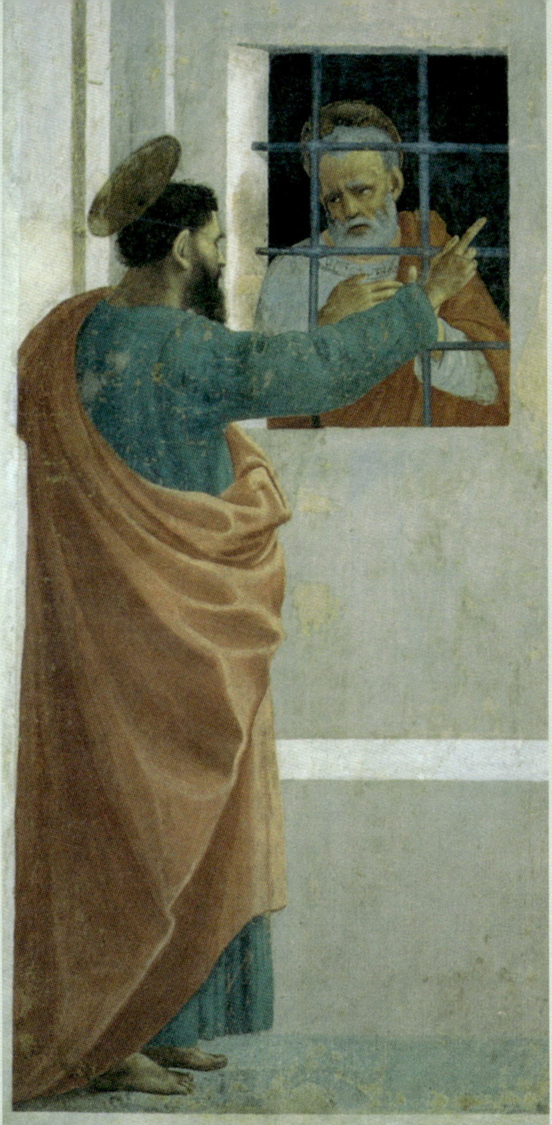

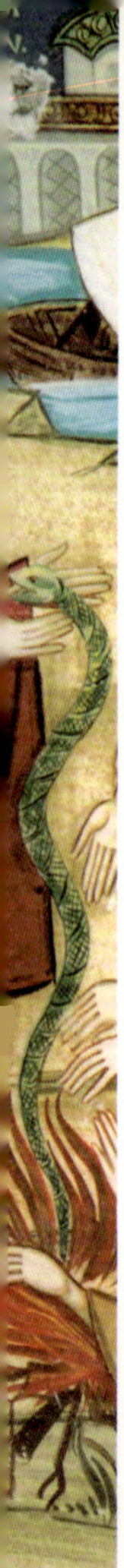

With perseverance

I want you to know how I strive for you,
for those of Laodicea
and for so many who have not met me personally.

Colosians 2:1

How many times
have I found myself in danger of death!
Five times the Jews sentenced me
to thirty-nine lashes.
Three times I was beaten with a rod,
once I was stoned.
Three times I was shipwrecked,
and once I spent a night and a day
adrift on the high seas.
Besides these and other things
there was my daily concern for all the churches.
Whoever wavers, do I not waver with him?
Whoever stumbles, am I not on hot bricks?
If it is necessary to boast,
let me proclaim the occasions on which
I was found weak.

2 Corinthians 11:23-30

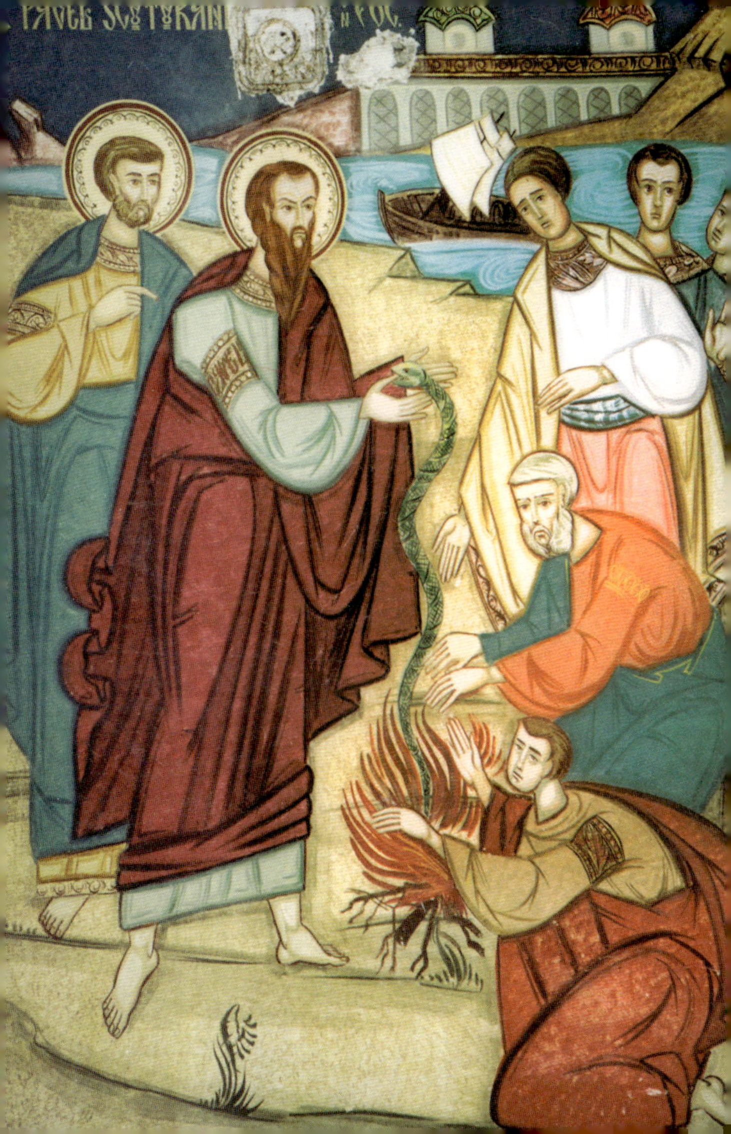

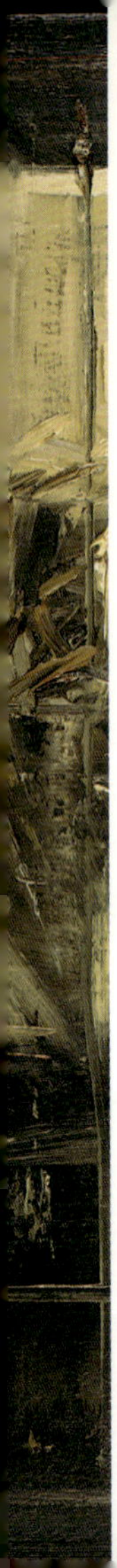

Always faithful

We prove we are true ministers of God
in every way by our endurance in so many trials,
in hardships, afflictions, floggings, imprisonment,
riots, fatigue, sleepless nights and days of hunger;
by our upright life, knowledge, patience and
kindness, action of the Holy Spirit, sincere love,
words of truth and power of God.
So we fight with the weapons of justice,
to attack as well as to defend.
Sometimes we are honoured,
at other times insulted;
we receive criticism as well as praise.
We are regarded as liars
although we speak the truth;
as unknown though we are well known;
as dead and yet we live.
Punishments come upon us
but we have not, as yet, been put to death.
We appear to be afflicted, yet always joyful;
we seem to be poor, but we enrich many;
we have nothing, but we possess everything.

2 Corinthians 6:4-10

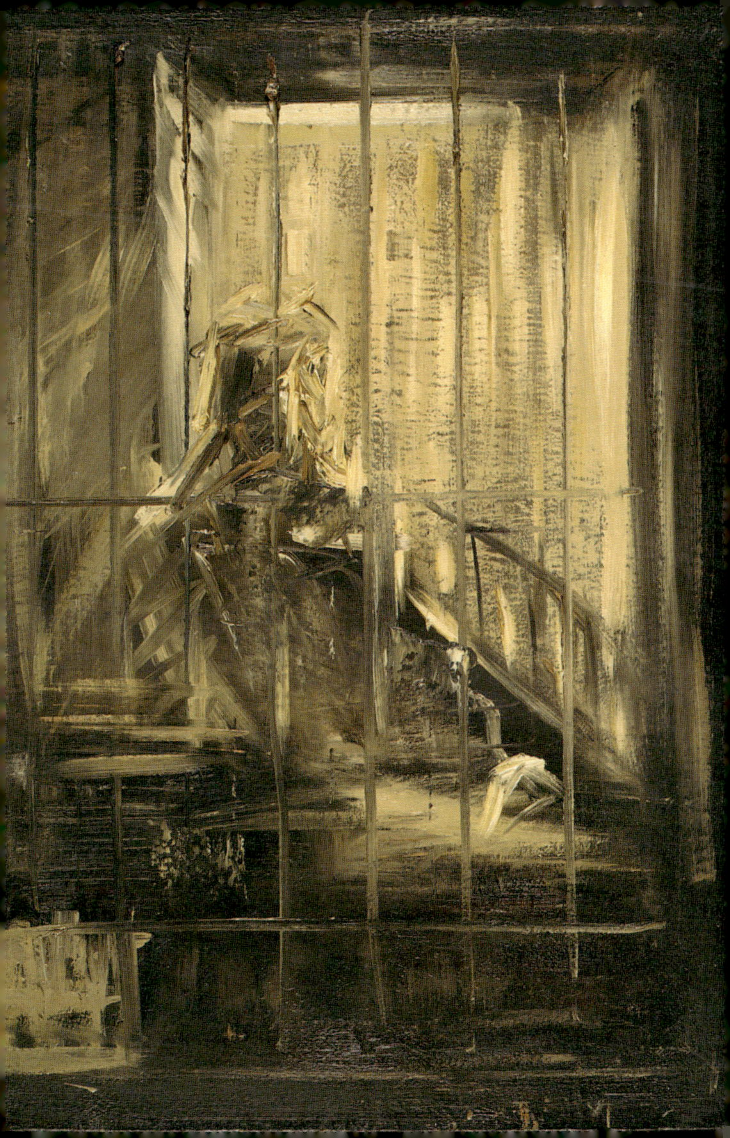

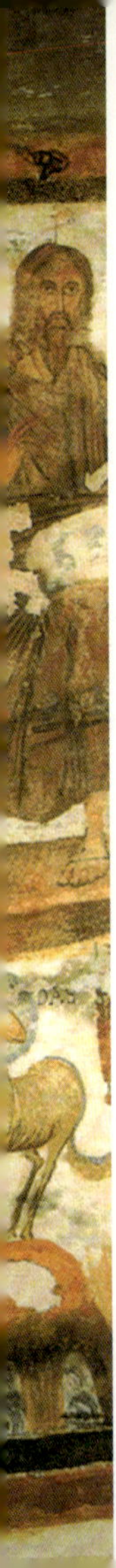

Straining forward

So, then, I run knowing where I go.
I box but not aimlessly in the air.
I punish my body and control it,
lest after preaching to others,
I myself should be rejected.

1 Corinthians 9:26-27

Forgetting what is behind me,
I race forward and run towards the goal,
my eyes on the prize to which
God has called us from above in Christ Jesus.

Philippians 3:13-14

As for me the time of sacrifice has arrived,
and the moment of my departure has come.
I have fought the good fight, I have finished the race,
I have kept the faith.
Now there is laid up for me
the crown of righteousness with which the Lord,
the just judge, will reward me on that day;
and not only me, but all those
who have longed for his glorious coming.

2 Timothy 4:6-8

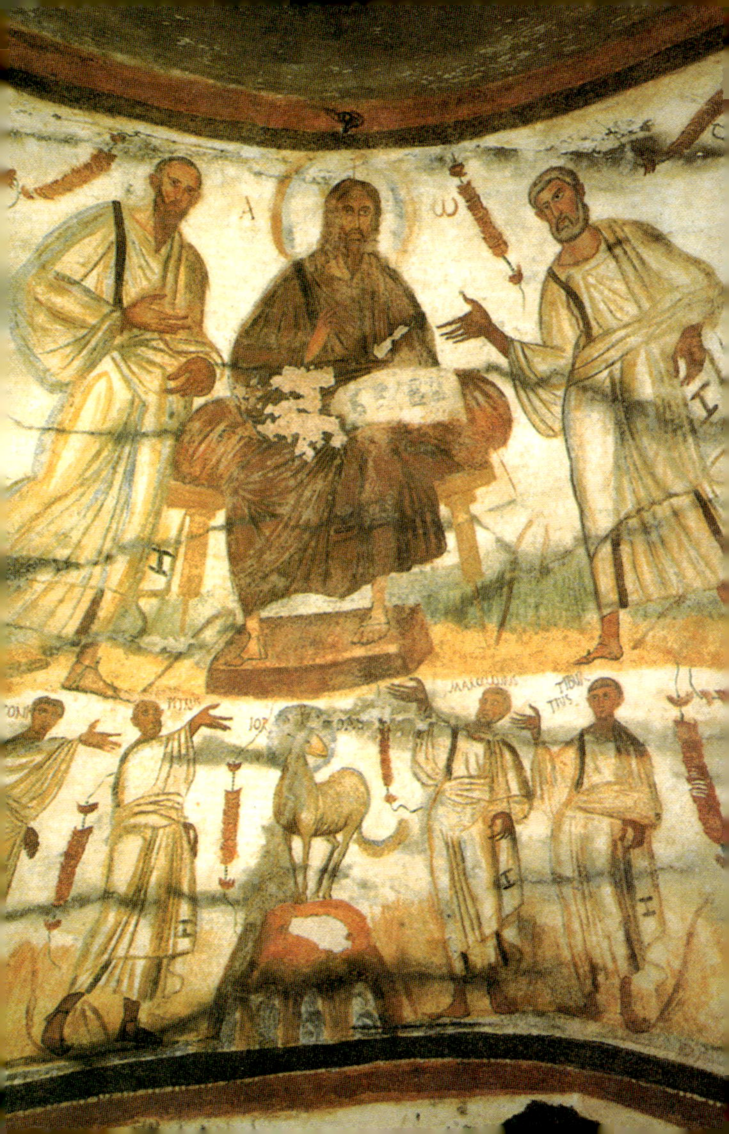

A
ω
IOR
TIBVR
TIVS

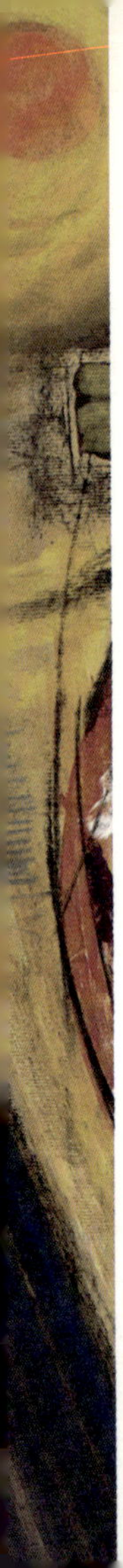

Praying with Paul...

With a grateful heart

I give thanks to my God each time I remember you,
and when I pray for you, I pray with joy.
I cannot forget all you shared with me
in the service of the Gospel,
from the first day until now.

Since God began such a good work in you,
I am certain that he will complete it
in the day of Christ Jesus.

This is my hope for you.
I carry you all in my heart...
God knows that I love you dearly
with the love of Christ Jesus.

In my prayers I ask that your love
may lead you each day to a deeper knowledge
and clearer discernment,
that you may have good criteria for everything
and come blameless to the day of Christ,
filled with the fruit of holiness
that comes through Christ Jesus,
for the glory and praise of God.

Philippians 1:3-11

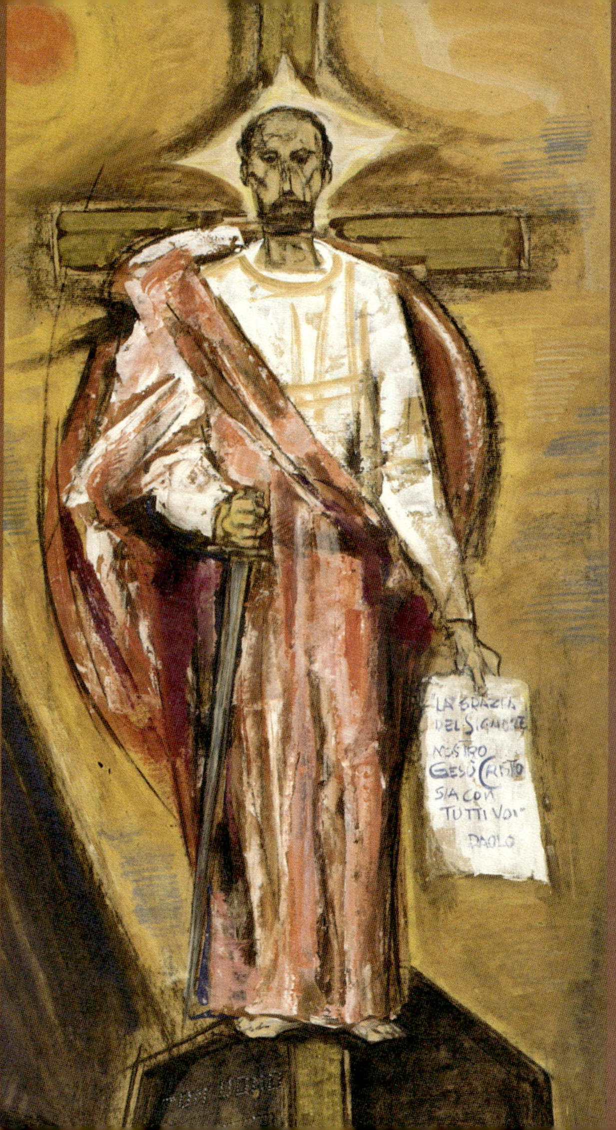
"LA GRAZIA
DEL SIGNORE
NOSTRO
GESÙ CRISTO
SIA CON
TUTTI VOI"
PAOLO

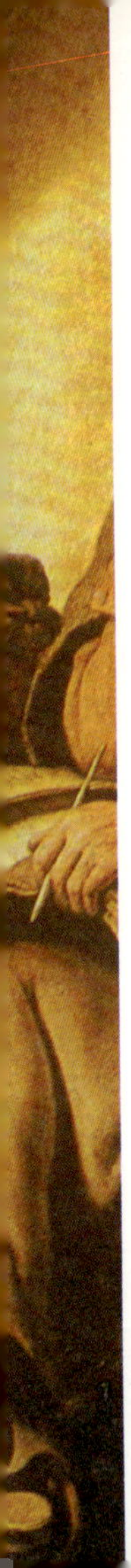

Praying with Paul...

The inner self

And now I kneel in the presence of the Father
from whom every family in heaven and on earth
has received its name.

May he strengthen in you the inner self
through his Spirit,
according to the riches of his glory;
may Christ dwell in your hearts through faith.

May you be rooted and founded in love.
All of this so that you may understand
with all the holy ones
the width, the length, the height and the depth–
in a word, that you may know the love of Christ
which surpasses all knowledge,
that you may be filled and reach the fullness of God.

Glory to God who shows his power in us
and can do much more than
we could ask or imagine;
glory to him in the Church and in Christ Jesus
through all generations for ever and ever.

Ephesians 3:14-21

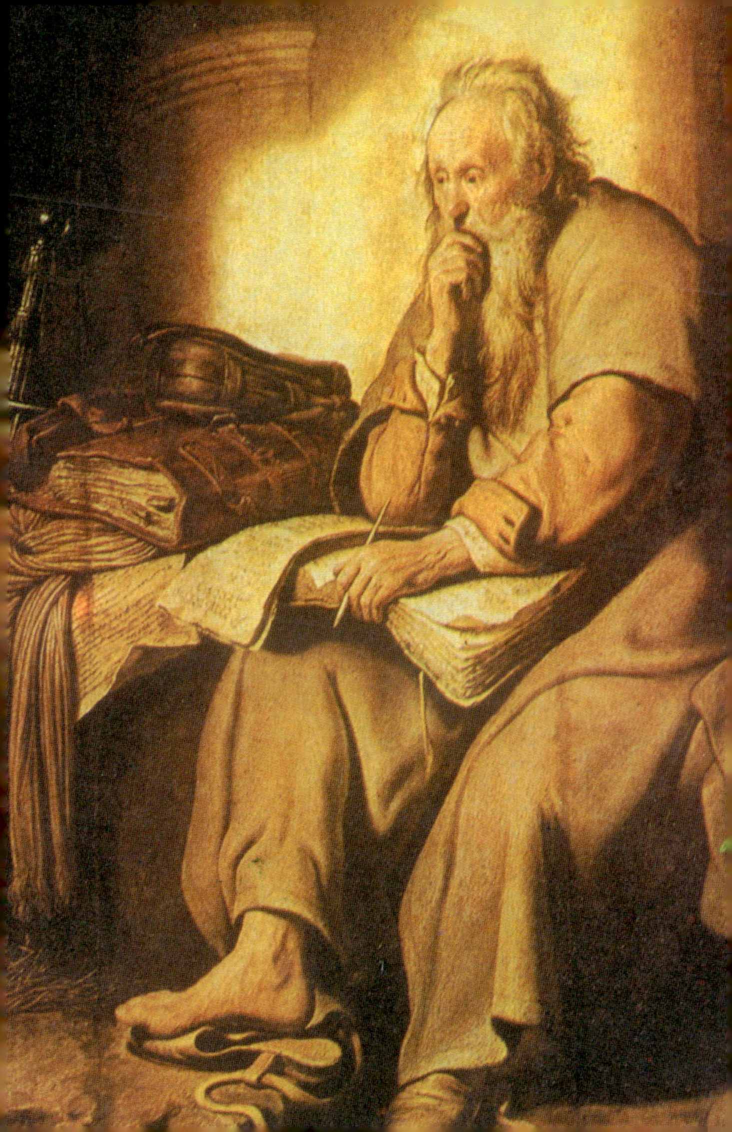

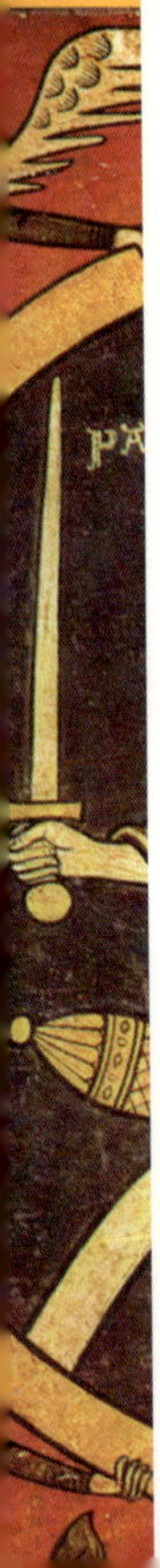

Praying with Paul...

A spirit of wisdom

I always give thanks to God,
remembering you in my prayers.

May the God of Christ Jesus our Lord,
the Father of Glory,
reveal himself to you
and give you a spirit of wisdom,
that you may know him.

May he enlighten your inner vision,
that you may appreciate
the things we hope for,
since we were called by God.

May you know
how great is the inheritance,
the glory God sets apart for his saints.
May you understand
with what extraordinary power he acts
in favour of us who believe.

Ephesians 1:16-19

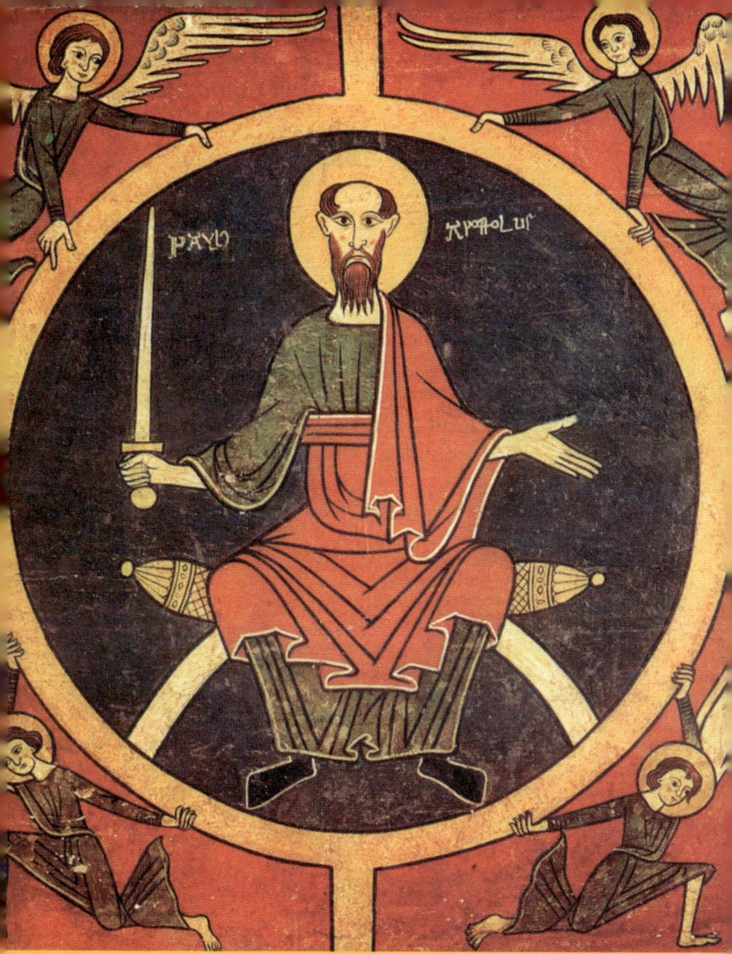

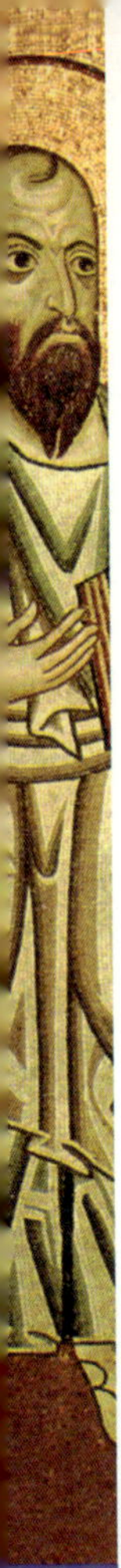

Praying with Paul...

Source of all comfort

Blessed be God, the Father of Christ Jesus, our Lord,
the all-merciful Father and the God of all comfort!
He encourages us in all our trials,
so that we may also encourage those in any trial,
with the same comfort that we receive from God.

For whenever the sufferings of Christ overflow to us,
so, through Christ, a great comfort also overflows.
So, if we are afflicted,
it is for your comfort and salvation;
and if we receive comfort it is also for you.

We want you to know
some of the trials we experienced...
We were crushed; it was too much;
it was more than we could bear and we had already
lost all hope of coming through alive.

... But his happened that we might no longer
rely on ourselves but on God...
We trust he will continue protecting us.

2 Corinthians 1:3-11

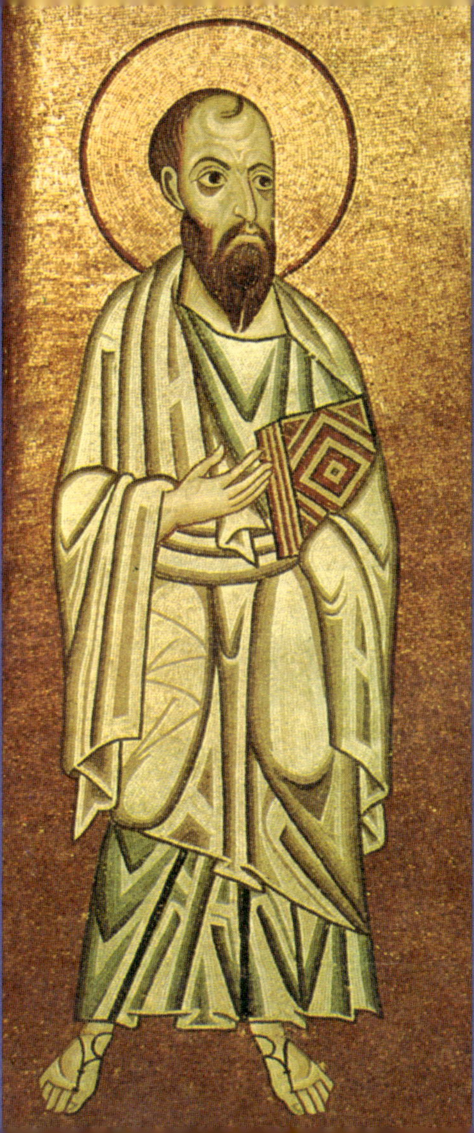

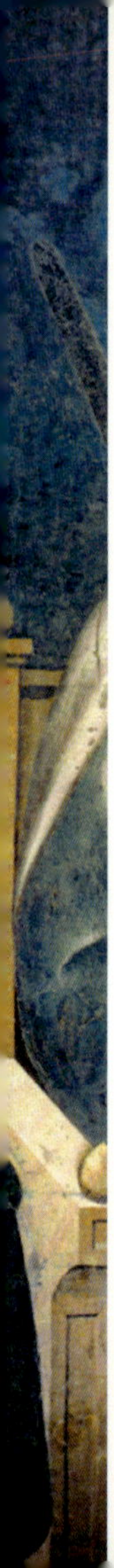

Praying with Paul...

Love

Strive, then, for love...

Love is patient, kind, without envy.
It is not boastful or arrogant.
It is not ill-mannered
nor does it seek its own interest.

Love overcomes anger
And forgets offenses.
It does not take delight in wrong,
But rejoices in truth.

Love excuses everything,
believes all things,
hopes all things,
endures all things.

Love will never end...
Now we have faith, hope and love,
these three,
but the greatest of these is love.

1 Corinthians 13:4-13

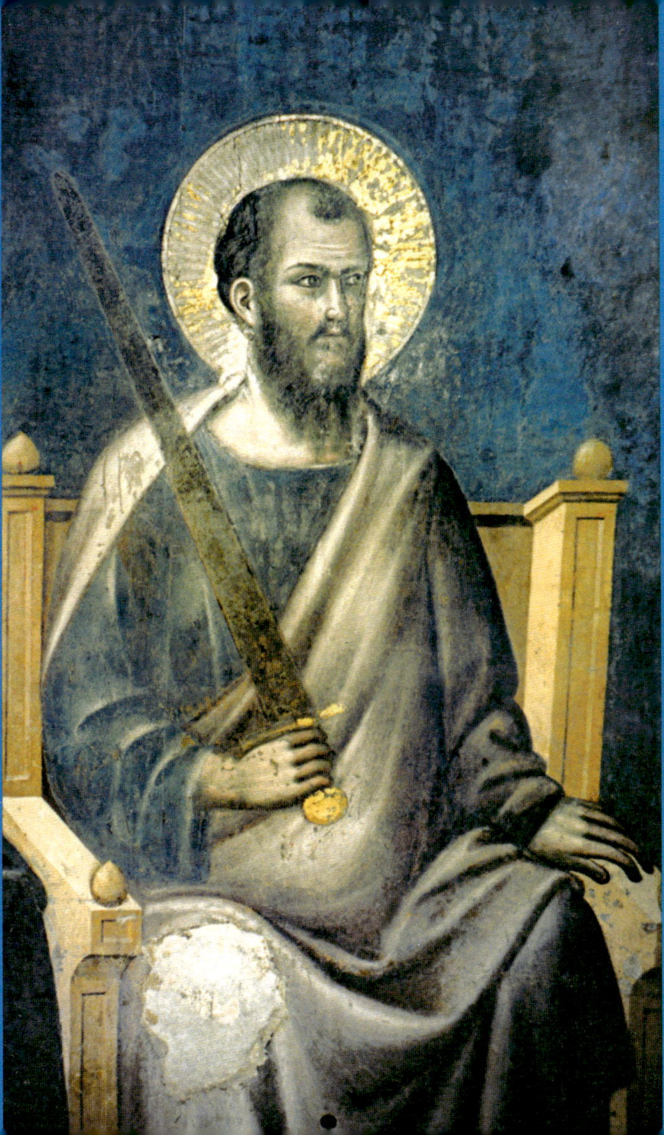

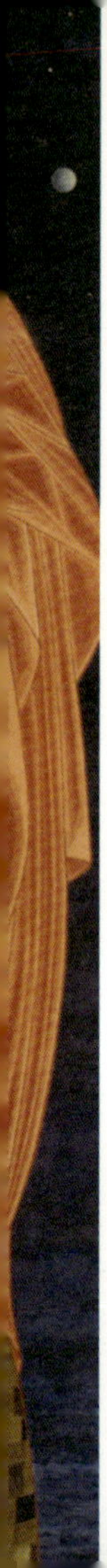

Paul alive today

All who call upon the name of the Lord
will be saved.
But how can they call upon the name of the Lord
without having believed in him?
And how can they believe in him
without having first heard about him?
And how will they hear about him
if no one preaches about him?
And how will they preach about him
if no one sends them?
As Scripture says:
How beautiful is
the coming of those who bring good news.

Romans 10:14-15

You are the answer.

If they are to call on his name,
if they are to become believers,
if they are to be saved,
then ***you*** *are the answer:*
Here I am Lord, send me!

Paintings

Probable chronology of Paul's life

1-10	Born at Tarsus
15-20	Studied at Jerusalem
36	Conversion
36-39	Damascus, Arabia, Jerusalem
39-43	Tarsus
43-44	Antioch
44-48	First missionary journey
49-50	Council of Jerusalem
	Confronts Peter at Antioch
49-53	Second missionary journey
51-52	Corinth – writes ***1*** and ***2 Thessalonians***
53-58	Third missionary journey
54	Ephesus – writes ***Galatians***
56	Ephesus – writes ***1 Corinthians***
57	Philippi – writes ***2 Corinthians***
57-58	Corinth – writes ***Romans***
58-60	Imprisoned in Cesarea
60-61	Journey to Rome
61-63	First imprisonment in Rome. Writes ***Ephesians, Colossians, Philemon, Philippians***
63-64	Journey to Spain
64-66	Journey to the East.
	Macedonia – writes ***1 Timothy***
66-67	Second imprisonment in Rome
	Writes ***2 Timothy***
67	Martyred in Rome

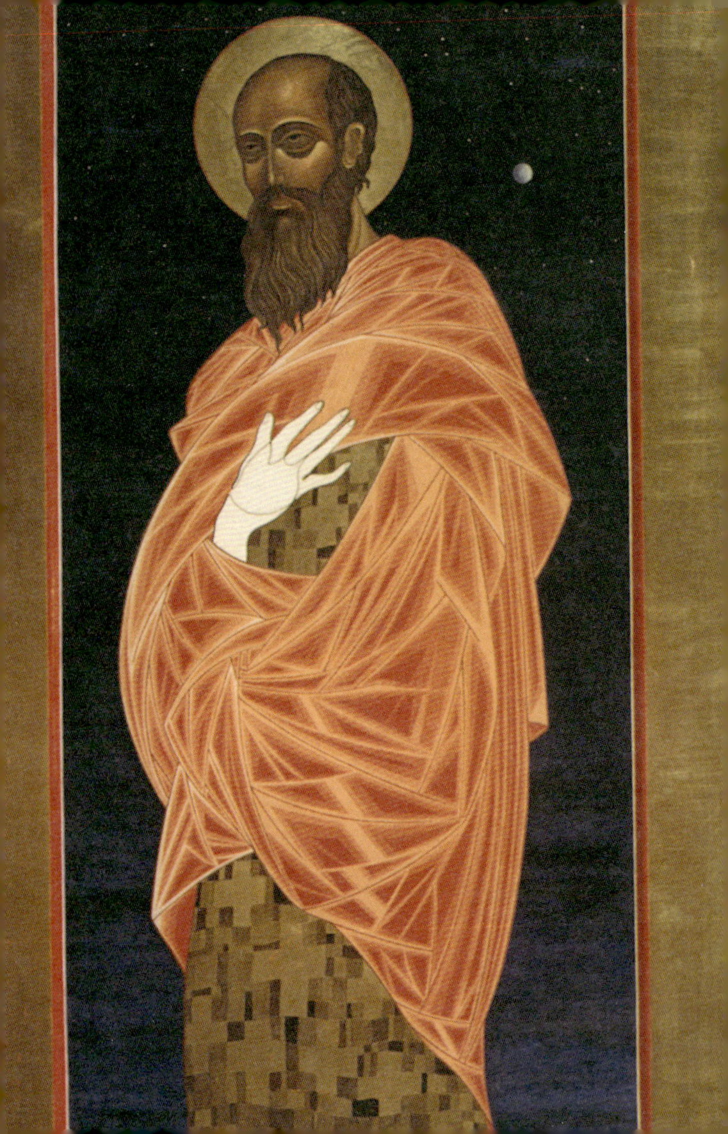